This book belongs to:

....

....

DREAM UNICORN COLORING BOOK FOR ADULTS

Coloring is one of the methods of learning and playing at the same
time, helping you to develop their vision, foster thinking ability,
observe and exercise the dexterity of their hands.
Dream Unicorn is an interesting choice for parents and children
to play together every day.

With funny drawings, bright colors, Dream Unicorn will be a close
companion for the little ones.

Parents should spend time to guide and encourage children when
they draw. After your child completes the works, you should
cheer and praise them to make them more excited. In addition,
you should also be careful in choosing safe paint colors for your baby.

Happy Coloring!

DREAM UNICORN COLORING BOOK FOR ADULTS

DREAM UNICORN COLORING BOOK FOR ADULTS

DREAM UNICORN COLORING BOOK FOR ADULTS

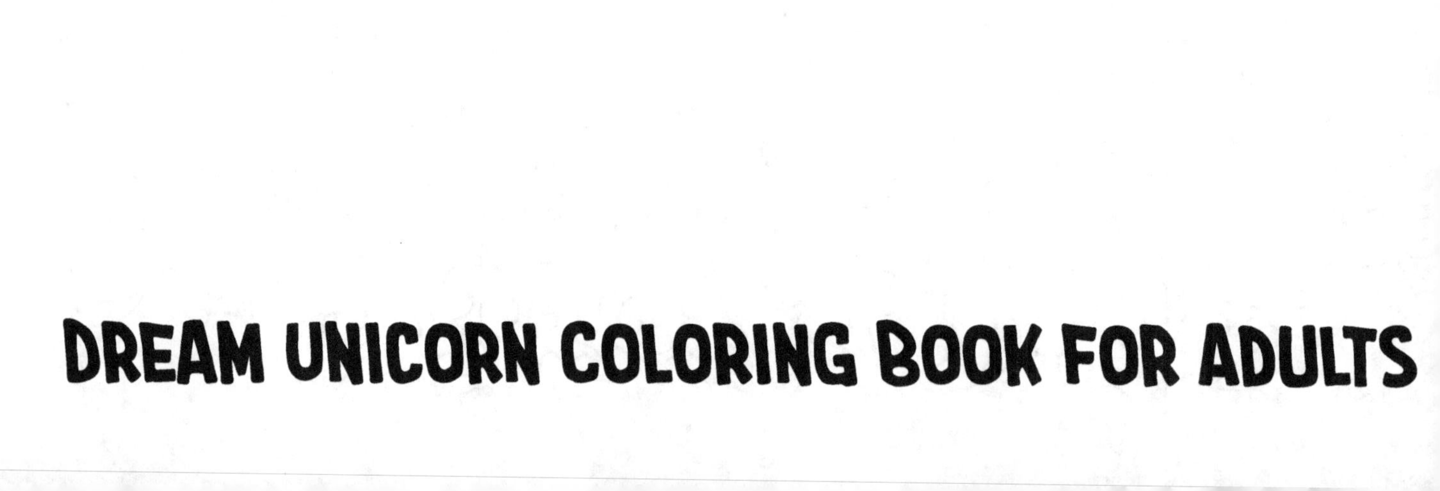
DREAM UNICORN COLORING BOOK FOR ADULTS

DREAM UNICORN COLORING BOOK FOR ADULTS

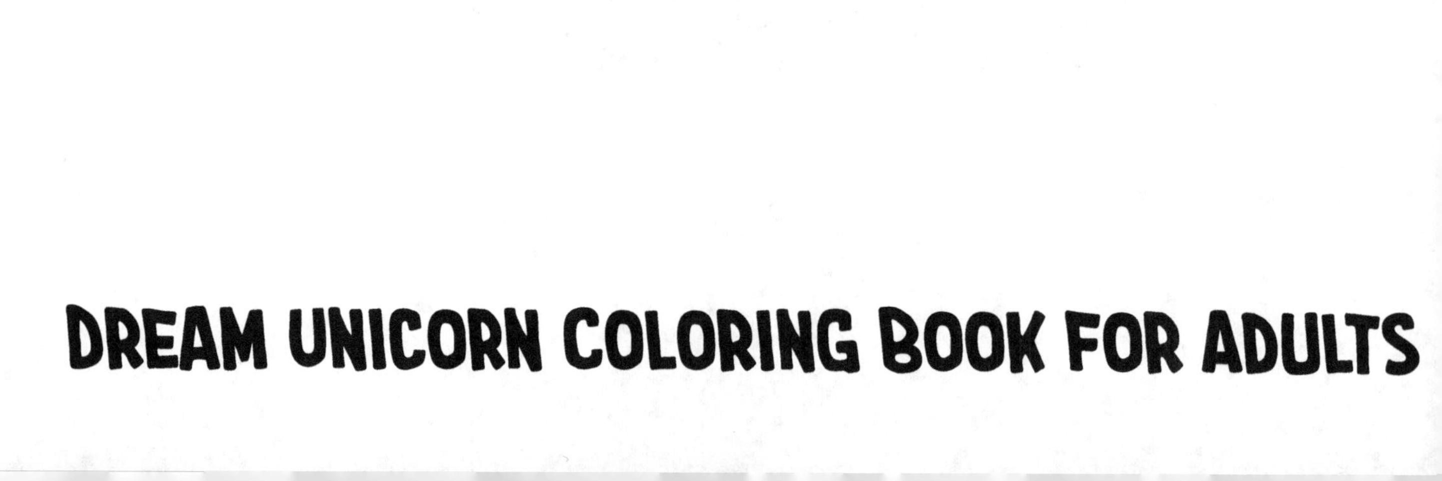

DREAM UNICORN COLORING BOOK FOR ADULTS

DREAM UNICORN COLORING BOOK FOR ADULTS

DREAM UNICORN COLORING BOOK FOR ADULTS

DREAM UNICORN COLORING BOOK FOR ADULTS

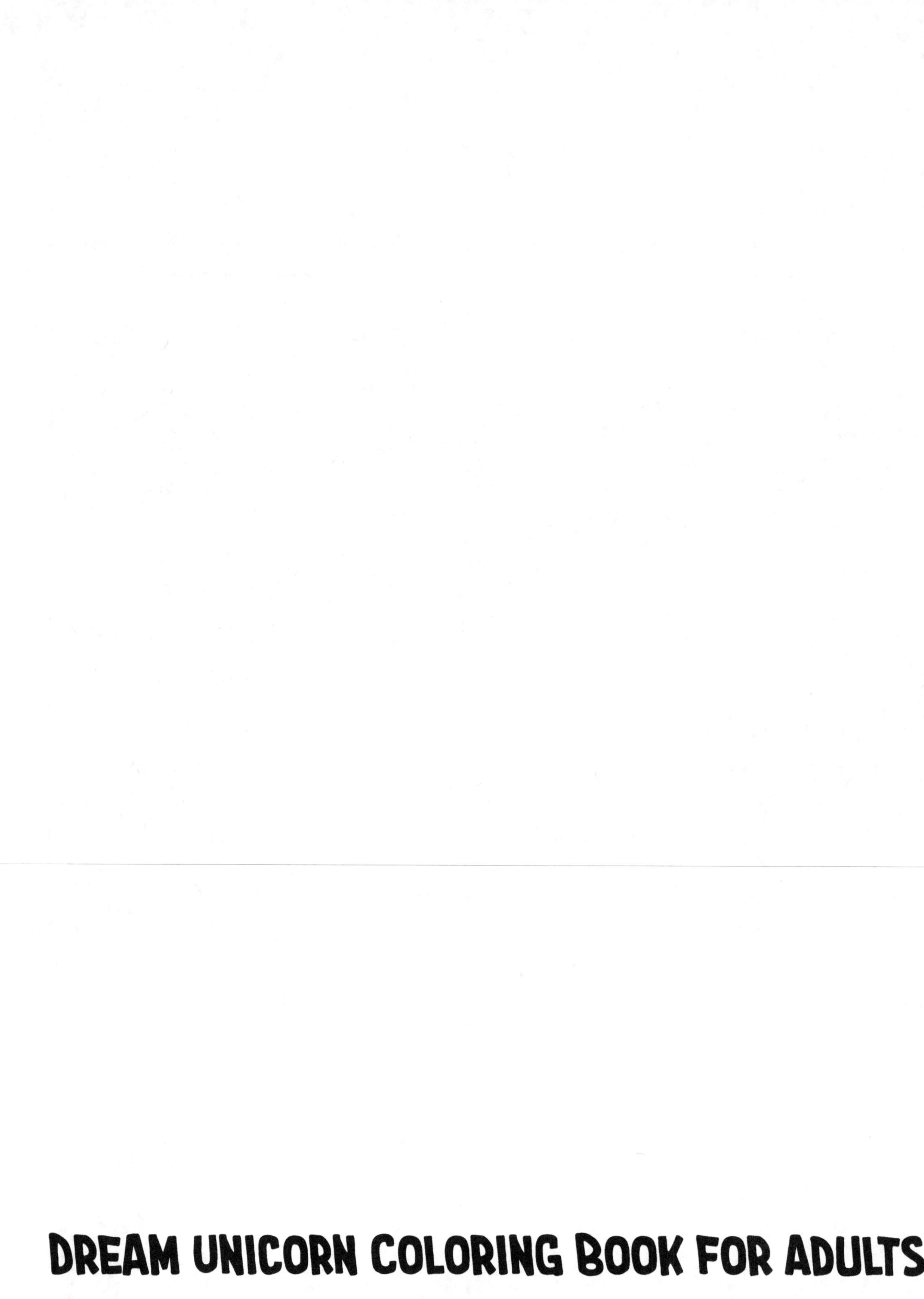

DREAM UNICORN COLORING BOOK FOR ADULTS

DREAM UNICORN COLORING BOOK FOR ADULTS

DREAM UNICORN COLORING BOOK FOR ADULTS

DREAM UNICORN COLORING BOOK FOR ADULTS

DREAM UNICORN COLORING BOOK FOR ADULTS

DREAM UNICORN COLORING BOOK FOR ADULTS

DREAM UNICORN COLORING BOOK FOR ADULTS

DREAM UNICORN COLORING BOOK FOR ADULTS

DREAM UNICORN COLORING BOOK FOR ADULTS

DREAM UNICORN COLORING BOOK FOR ADULTS

DREAM UNICORN COLORING BOOK FOR ADULTS

DREAM UNICORN COLORING BOOK FOR ADULTS

DREAM UNICORN COLORING BOOK FOR ADULTS

DREAM UNICORN COLORING BOOK FOR ADULTS

DREAM UNICORN COLORING BOOK FOR ADULTS

DREAM UNICORN COLORING BOOK FOR ADULTS

DREAM UNICORN COLORING BOOK FOR ADULTS

DREAM UNICORN COLORING BOOK FOR ADULTS

DREAM UNICORN COLORING BOOK FOR ADULTS

DREAM UNICORN COLORING BOOK FOR ADULTS

DREAM UNICORN COLORING BOOK FOR ADULTS

www.ingramcontent.com/pod-product-compliance
Lightning Source LLC
Chambersburg PA
CBHW081745250726
48657CB00010B/3412